A Walk
and a Prayer

Glimpsing God
in the World around Us

A WALK AND A PRAYER
Glimpsing God in the World around Us

Copyright © 2006 Nick Fawcett
Original edition published in English under the title A WALK
AND A PRAYER by Kevin Mayhew Ltd, Buxhall, England.
This edition copyright © Fortress Press 2019

All rights reserved. Except for brief quotations in critical articles or
reviews, no part of this book may be reproduced in any manner
without prior written permission from the publisher. Email
copyright@augsburgfortress.org or write to Permissions, Fortress
Press, PO Box 1209, Minneapolis, MN 55440-1209.

Cover image: Cover photo by strelov from iStock
Cover design: Emily Wyland

Print ISBN: 978-1-5064-5906-6

Contents

Introduction	4
The Mountain Spring	5
The Beach	6
The Pebble	7
The Tide	8
The Sea Stack	9
The Seagull	10
The Grassy Bank	11
The Bluebell Woods	12
The Blossom	13
The Oak Tree	14
The Fallen Tree	15
The Lichen	16
The Berries	17
The Thistle	18
The City Park	19
The Sparrow	20
The Kestrel	21
The Swallows	22
The Feather	23
The Molehill	24
The Spider's Web	25
The Landslip	26
The Sunburn	27
The Shadow	28
The Breeze	29
The Storm Clouds	30
The Shelter	31
The Snowflake	32

Introduction

"See how the wildflowers grow," said Jesus; "pay heed to them. They do not labor or weave, yet I can assure you that not even Solomon in all his grandeur was decked out like one of these." Those words, and others like them, show that Jesus knew, as well as any, that the natural world can speak of God, pointing beyond itself to deeper realities. Not, of course, that we can prove God's existence from it, for there is probably as much in nature that argues against as in support of his presence, but to the eye of faith there is much nonetheless that speaks in a special way of something beyond us. Certainly there are few times when I personally feel closer to God than when out roaming the countryside; many of my recent books, including the three that this compilation is drawn from, have largely been written during lunchtime walks.

The prayers in this book draw inspiration from the sort of things you might see during just such a walk, whether in rain or sunshine, summer or winter; through woods or fields, by the sea or deep in a city. The sight of a seagull or a tree in blossom, the touch of the breeze or fall of a snowflake, the grandeur of a tree or gurgle of a mountain spring—each here is offered as the starting point for deeper reflection, in the hope that you too may glimpse more of God in the everyday sights and sounds around us each day.

Nick Fawcett

The Mountain Spring

It bubbled up,
   sparkling and irrepressible,
   gurgling with delight as it cascaded down the hillside,
   and I stooped to drink,
   marveling at its taste,
   the water cool and clear,
   never running dry.

Your love, Lord, wells up the same,
   day upon day,
   year upon year,
   an unfailing spring of living water,
   poured out beyond my deserving,
   so that my cup overflows.
For your faithful blessing,
   so freely given,
   so joyfully received,
   receive my praise.

Amen.

The Beach

I ran the sand through my fingers, Lord,
  millions of grains,
  yet that one handful was just a fraction of what made up the beach,
  the beach one of thousands across the world,
  and the world itself merely a tiny speck in the vastness of space
  with its trillions of constellations and plethora of galaxies.

It leaves me reeling, Lord,
  such magnitude truly awesome,
  yet you brought it all into being,
  sustaining it each day
  and leading it toward fulfillment,
  the universe and everything within it the work of your hands.
As you created the stars and the sand,
  so you have fashioned our lives—
  knowing us better than we know ourselves,
  calling us by name,
  loving us more than we can begin to fathom.
For the vastness of your purpose,
  the immensity of your creation
  and the mind-boggling wonder of your grace,
  Lord, thank you.

Amen.

The Pebble

It was perfectly smooth,
  the fissures and fractures it had once held
  long since worn away by the pounding of waves
  and ceaseless jostling of its fellows,
  each stone helping to round the next.

Lord, I too need the company of others to remove rough
  edges,
  the experience of rubbing shoulders with people of different
  backgrounds, ideas, and experiences,
  if I'm to become fully rounded.
Open my heart to those around me,
  and in our bouncing off each other,
  the interaction we enjoy,
  shape our lives for good.

Amen.

The Tide

It was a sea of mud now,
    haven to a host of waders probing for tasty titbits;
    a bleak and desolate expanse,
    haunting and mournful.
Yet already the tide was turning,
    the scene soon to be a sea of blue once more,
    shimmering in the sunlight,
    splashing on the shore;
    a haven for boats bobbing on the swell
    and children paddling among the waves.
Day in, day out,
    like a gentle pulse,
    it rises and falls,
    ebbs and flows.

For me too, Lord, life brings its ups and downs.
Remind me that they belong together,
    each a part of the greater whole,
    and teach me to trust you through both the highs and lows,
    sensing through it all the rhythm of your grace
    and heartbeat of your love.

Amen.

The Sea Stack

It looked so solid,
  so permanent,
  standing tall and proud against the waves,
  certain to be there still when I am long gone,
  defying the march of time.
But all was not as it seemed,
  for that rock—
  once a cliff,
  once a mountain—
  was destined to become a boulder,
  pebble,
  stone,
  and, finally, a grain of sand,
  before, who could say, being thrust up again in eons to come,
  the whole process beginning again.

Only you, Lord, do not change,
  your love eternal,
  your mercy constant,
  your purpose enduring.
Teach me in this shifting world,
  here today and gone tomorrow,
  to trust in you,
  the same now and always.

Amen.

The Seagull

It rose effortlessly on the breeze,
  instinctively catching the rising air—
  first this current,
  then another—
  gliding,
  swooping,
  climbing,
  diving,
  riding the thermals with casual assurance and exuberant
  delight.

Lord, release me from the chains that shackle me to
  this world,
  encumbering my mind and imprisoning my spirit.
Grant me a deeper knowledge of the truth that sets me free,
  that I might rise on wings of faith
  and soar in the light of your love,
  celebrating the glorious liberty your grace bestows.

Amen.

The Grassy Bank

It was nothing special,
   just an ordinary bank of grass,
   no different from the meadow in which they stood,
   yet the cows were straining to nibble it,
   heads thrusting eagerly through the fence
   as though there were no tomorrow
   and this was the choicest of feasts.

I laughed, Lord,
   but I shouldn't have,
   for though I know it's foolish,
   I too assume the grass is greener on the other side,
   time after time coveting what I do not have
   and hankering for what I cannot reach,
   as though I'm somehow missing out on what others around
   me enjoy.
Teach me, instead, to count my blessings,
   more than I can number,
   and to be content.

Amen.

The Bluebell Woods

What a sight!
What a scent!
What an unforgettable picture they made!
Soon over, it's true,
   but for the month they were in bloom,
   each delicate head nodding in the breeze,
   they turned the woodland into an ocean of color
   and fragrance,
   a glimpse of Eden,
   a foretaste of paradise I will never forget.

Lord, our human span,
   like the bluebell's,
   is all too brief,
   in the context of the universe just a passing moment,
   a fleeting shadow.
Help me to make the most of the time you give me,
   living each moment to the full
   and, in my own small way,
   reflecting something of your love and glory,
   until that day when I do not merely glimpse paradise
   but behold it in all its glory.

Amen.

The Blossom

I stood spellbound by its beauty:
   a fragrant cloud of blossom transforming what had seemed an ordinary tree
     into something breathtaking,
     unforgettable.
Entrancing in itself,
   it promised fruit to come,
   a rich harvest in the making.

Lord, there is little harvest in my life,
   and that which there has been is nothing special.
But if fruits are missing,
   may there at least be blossom,
   some sign of future growth;
   and though I will always fall short,
   may something of your beauty be seen in me.

Amen.

The Oak Tree

It stood solid and strong,
    its gnarled and knotted roots protruding through the ground like swollen veins,
    sustaining the life that coursed through the mighty trunk and twisted branches.
Through wind, rain, drought, and frost, it had stood defiant,
    its vigor undiminished,
    and no doubt it will see out centuries to come,
    as it has centuries gone by.

Lord, anchor my life in your love,
    your word,
    your will,
    that I too may be able to resist the trials life throws against me.
Nurture my faith and strengthen my commitment,
    so that whatever turmoil I face,
    whatever testing endure,
    when all has done its worst I may still stand tall,
    unbowed,
    unbroken.

Amen.

The Fallen Tree

It was hard to believe—
    the mighty tree that had stood for so long,
felled by the gale—
    yet the proof was there before me,
    the roots laid bare,
    trunk prostrate,
    branches smashed and splintered.
Its strength had been its undoing,
    for, unable to bend,
    it had caught the full force of the wind
    and been sent crashing to the ground.

Teach me, Lord, that though at times I need to stand firm,
    unyielding on matters of faith and principle,
    at other times I must be ready to give a little,
    recognizing my limitations,
    open to new insights,
    and bowing to the wisdom of others.
Help me to know which time is which,
    and give me, as appropriate,
    courage or humility to do both.

Amen.

The Lichen

How it grew there was beyond me,
   for it was bare rock—
   rough,
   windswept,
   barren—
   yet the lichen had colonized its surface:
   nothing fancy or luxuriant,
   but eking out a living,
   somehow surviving against all odds.

It reminded me, Lord, that so many in this world simply **survive**,
   struggling each day to get by as best they can.
Not for them the trappings of life we take for granted,
   the accoutrements we see as ours by right—
   they are happy to find even the essentials,
   let alone more.
Help me to remember how lucky I am,
   how much I have to celebrate,
   and teach me to respond,
   generously and lovingly,
   so that others may flourish in turn.

Amen.

The Berries

They looked good,
   succulent and tasty,
   and for the birds, at least, they were just that,
   a welcome meal through the lean months of winter.
But, of course, appearances deceived,
   any meal I made of them likely to be my last.

Teach me, Lord, not to be taken in by what looks appealing
   but finally destroys,
   what promises satisfaction
   yet ultimately poisons within.
However enticing temptation may be,
   help me to see where it might lead
   and to avoid its hidden dangers.

Amen.

The Thistle

A weed some called it,
  but it wasn't really:
  it was simply a wildflower growing in cultivated ground,
  possessing its own exquisite beauty for those with eyes
  to see,
  but, not fitting into the gardener's plan,
  it was grubbed out with barely a second thought.

Lord, not everything or everyone is to my liking,
  for, like anyone else, I have my own ideas of what's pleasing
    and good.
But save me from dismissing the worth of that which doesn't fit
  my criteria.
Help me to respect the value of others,
  and their right to see things differently than I do;
  to understand that beauty is in the eye of the beholder,
  and that, just because I fail to see it,
  doesn't mean it isn't there.

Amen.

The City Park

It was such a surprise:
   there, so close to the roar of traffic and milling crowds,
   the jostling skyscrapers and throb of city life,
   a little park,
   an oasis of tranquillity,
   a quiet retreat from the hectic world beyond.
Flowers bloomed,
   trees blossomed,
   birds sang,
   squirrels played,
   oblivious to the incongruity of it all.

The peace you promise, Lord, is equally unlikely
   yet just as real,
   not removed from this world
   but found equally amid the hurly-burly of life,
   the stresses and strains of the daily routine.
Open my heart, Lord, to that special peace beyond
   understanding,
   and may it touch each moment of every day.

Amen.

The Sparrow

I caught the movement as I crouched in the hide—
   a sudden flutter of wings—
   and, grabbing my binoculars, I scanned the trees,
   excited and expectant,
   straining to catch a sight . . .
   but then . . . disappointment . . . dismay,
   for it was nothing interesting,
   nothing rare . . .
   only a sparrow.

Only a sparrow?
What do I mean, Lord?
It may be plain,
   but, like everything else in the world,
   it's a miracle,
   a wonder,
   special beyond words—
   each bone and feather a work of art,
   fashioned by your hands and speaking of you.
However ordinary it may seem or familiar be,
   teach me never to lose my sense of wonder at all you have made.

Amen.

The Kestrel

It hovered overhead,
　scanning the ground below for movement,
　eyes only for the task at hand,
　all else blotted out.
Though the wind gusted and rain fell,
　though children played and cars raced by,
　it hung there still,
　motionless,
　focused,
　immune to all distractions.

Give me, Lord, a similar focus on you,
　the ability to concentrate my thoughts in daily devotion
　and faithful discipleship,
　making you the center of all I do and am,
　the hub of my life and goal of all my being.
Whatever temptations and pressures I face,
　may nothing distract me from knowing you better
　and responding in grateful, loving service.

Amen.

The Swallows

They perched on the phone wires,
   hundreds assembled there,
   as though they'd been summoned for duty,
   commanded to prepare for action.
And in a sense they had,
   each responding to the call of the wild,
   an irresistible pull that would see them soon depart,
   embarking on another epic journey to warmer climes.

I can't explain your call, Lord,
   for there's so much about it I don't understand,
   so much about you,
   about faith,
   about life itself,
   that leaves me searching for answers;
   troubled, confused, uncertain.
And yet, though I don't have all the answers,
   I know that your summons rings true,
   your invitation to know and love you finding an echo in my heart,
   answering some primal need deep within;
   and until I respond I can find no rest.
Help me, fully and faithfully, to commit myself to you
   and to follow where you might lead.

Amen.

The Feather

It fell from the sky,
   fluttering gently on the breeze,
   before landing in the palm of my hand
   with a touch so soft it barely registered.
Yet that same feather had helped carry a bird in flight,
   bearing its weight as wings strained against the wind,
   deceptive strength behind such apparent fragility.

Grant me, Lord, a similar combination:
   strength of faith, character, wisdom, and purpose
   coupled with a gentleness of spirit;
   an inner steel
   matched by tenderness and humility in my dealings with others.
Though I am weak,
   may I be strong in you.

Amen.

The Molehill

It looked a mess,
  the lawn ruined,
  months of raking, mowing, feeding, and weeding undermined   overnight.
But the damage was superficial,
  easily enough put right,
  in a few weeks rectified as though it had never been.

There are molehills in my life, Lord—
  problems, trials, and disagreements that get under my skin—
  but most of them are minor rather than major,
  a nuisance,
  nothing more.
Forgive me for turning them into mountains,
  magnifying them out of all proportion
  until I can see nothing else.
Give me, Lord, in all things, a proper sense of perspective,
  lest the biggest problem I face is **me**.

Amen.

The Spider's Web

It looked pathetically frail,
   the silken threads likely to snap at the slightest pressure,
   yet, as a hapless fly had found,
   the truth was very different,
   the web like a steel cage,
   escape impossible once snared in its embrace.

Teach me, Lord, never to underestimate your strength,
   even when it looks like weakness;
   never to lose sight of the power of love,
   the might of truth,
   or the force of good,
   however much hatred, falsehood, or evil may conspire
   against them.
Remind me that nothing in heaven or earth,
   the present or the future,
   will finally be able to frustrate your purpose,
   for you are able to turn sorrow to joy,
   darkness to light,
   and death to life—
   your love stronger than all.

Amen.

The Landslip

They looked impregnable,
   mighty cliffs rearing magnificently from the water,
   towering over all they surveyed.
But the battle between sea and rock was one-sided,
   each year another few feet eaten away,
   the waves nibbling relentlessly,
   changing the coastal scene year upon year.

I like to think my faith is impregnable, Lord,
   able to stand up to whatever life may throw against it.
But it's not.
It too is remorselessly attacked,
   imperceptibly eroded over the years.
The assault may not be obvious,
   sometimes indeed too small even to notice,
   but the temptation to compromise
   and pressure to give in
   insidiously gnaw away at my commitment,
   until it is barely recognizable,
   a shadow of what it used to be.
Strengthen my faith
and defend me against all that conspires against it.

Amen.

The Sunburn

I should have covered up,
  or splashed on the sun cream,
  but I didn't
  and paid the price,
  that extra halfhour in the sun being a halfhour too much,
  turning a healthy tan into an ugly burn,
  a moment's pleasure into a week of pain.

So much in life, Lord, is special
  when enjoyed in moderation,
  but I indulge to excess,
  time and again craving that little bit more,
  rarely content with what I have.
Remind me that we can all have too much of a good thing,
  and help me to recognize when enough is enough.

Amen.

The Shadow

A shadow fell across us
   and the world felt darker,
   the air suddenly cool,
   yet the sun was still shining,
   as bright and warm as ever,
   the shade cast **because** of its presence,
   not despite it.

Remind me, Lord, that,
   in this life,
   there can be no sun without shadow
   or laughter without tears,
   and that sometimes the darkness seems deeper the more
   the light shines.
Teach me, then, however dark the shade,
   to keep faith,
   trusting that, despite appearances,
   you are there.

Amen.

The Breeze

It caressed my cheek, gentle and soothing,
  offering welcome relief from the heat of the noontime sun,
  and then it was gone to heaven knows where.
What stories could it tell?
What places had it seen?
What forms taken, lives touched, paths followed?
Had it raged in a tropical storm,
  whipped up desert sand,
  or whistled over polar ice sheet?
Had it sped yachtsmen across the ocean,
  lifted eagles high above mountain peaks,
  sent leaves cascading from bronze-leafed woodland?
Or was this the start of a new journey,
  the tranquil air stirring from silent slumber to wild wakefulness?

Lord, remind me that I can no more fathom the workings of
  your mind
  than control the course of the wind;
  that I can never know, still less dictate,
  where and when you will move,
  or in what ways and among whom you may choose to act.
Open my life to whatever you would do,
  wherever, whenever, and however you choose to do it.

Amen.

The Storm Clouds

They changed everything, those clouds, in an instant—
  one moment the world bathed in light
  and the next a shadow over all,
  one moment full of warmth
  and the next a brooding chill.
Thunder rumbled,
  lightning streaked the sky,
  and the storm broke in wild fury . . .
  and then it was gone,
  skies bright once more,
  threat replaced by promise,
  sunshine after rain.

Remind me, Lord, in the storms of life,
  when the clouds hang heavy and the world seems dark,
  that your light continues to shine though all seems in turmoil.
Teach me, however distant you may seem,
  still to trust you,
  assured that your love will break through
  and its radiance enfold me once more.

Amen.

The Shelter

They'd hardly noticed it before,
   passing it by with barely a glance,
   but when the storm broke and the rain lashed down,
   they noticed it **then**
   and huddled hurriedly inside,
   grateful for its cover.

I'm forgetful of **you**, Lord, much of the time,
   paying you scant heed until trouble strikes,
   only then remembering your love
   and running for shelter in your protective arms,
   a refuge in time of need.
Yet though I ignore you for so long,
   always you are ready to welcome,
   as faithful as I am fickle.
Thank you, Lord, for being there,
   come what may.

Amen.

The Snowflake

Are they really **all** different,
  these innumerable flakes each distinctive,
  unlike every other?
It seems impossible,
  yet that's what they say,
  every one of them unique,
  each having, however small, some distinguishing characteristic,
  an inimitable pattern that sets it apart.

Remind me, Lord, that people also are different,
  no two precisely the same;
  that though we all have some things in common with others,
  none of us can simply be lumped together,
  labeled as being of a certain type or particular kind.
Teach me to recognize the individuality of all
  and to respect each person I meet for who they are.

Amen.

www.ingramcontent.com/pod-product-compliance
Lightning Source LLC
Chambersburg PA
CBHW052038070526
44584CB00020B/3151